SAYILARIN HİKAYESİ

THE NUMBER STORY

SMALL BOOK ONE

ENGLISH - TURKISH

*Numbers Teach Children
Their Number Names*

written and illustrated by

MISS ANNA

Early Reader Edition of *The Number Story 1*
Bronze Medal Winner, 2016 Wishing Shelf Book Award

Library of Congress Control Number: 2018902040

Names: Miss Anna, author.
Title: Number story : numbers teach children their number names / Miss Anna.
Description: Portland, OR: Lumpy Publishing, 2018.
Identifiers: ISBN 978-1-945977-43-5| LCCN 2018902040
Summary: The pictures and rhymes present stories which introduce numbers 0-10.
Subjects: LCSH Numeration—English--Turkish--Pictorial works--Juvenile literature. | BISAC JUVENILE NONFICTION /
Languages: English--Turkish
Classification: LCC QA141.3 .M57 2018 | DDC 513—dc23

Publisher: Lumpy Publishing
Website: www.missannabooks.com
Email: missanna@missannabooks.com

Paperback: ISBN 978-1-945977-43-5
Printed in the U.S.A.   1 3 5 7 9 10 8 6 4 2

Sayıların ismini

öğrenmek ister misin?

It is very easy and a lot of fun!

Çok kolay ve çok eğlencelidir!

Say-along our little jingle

Küçük şarkımızı birlikte söyleyelim!

starting from Number One!

Bir sayısıyla başlıyoruz!

1
ONE   looks like my one finger.
BİR
Bir parmağıma benzer.

ONE!
BİR!

2

TWO trails a tail.

İKİ

İki'nin bir kuyruğu var.

A TAIL! BIR KUYRUK!

3

THREE   has bumps.

ÜÇ

Üç'ün tepeleri var.

BUMPY! TEPELI!

4

FOUR carries a sail.

DÖRT

Dört'ün üzerinde bir yelkeni var.

4
A SAIL!
BIR YELKEN!

5
FIVE   is a racing track.
BEŞ
Beş bir yarış pistidir.

VROOM
Vinnn Vinnn!

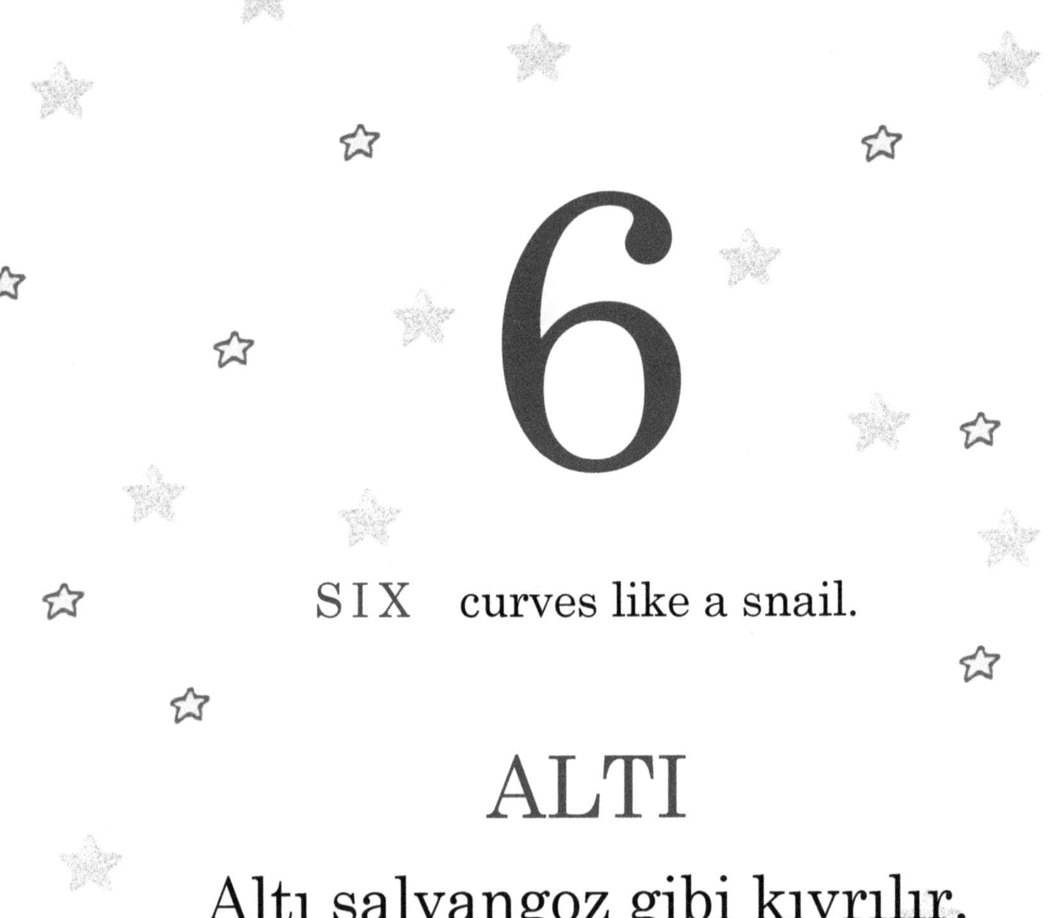

6

S I X   curves like a snail.

ALTI

Altı salyangoz gibi kıvrılır.

A SNAIL! BIR SALYANGOZ!

7

SEVEN has a sharp angle.

YEDİ

Yedi'nin keskin bir köşesi var.

OUCH!
OOO!

8

EIGHT is rollercoaster rails.

SEKİZ

Sekiz eğlence treni raylarıdır.

YUPPİ!
YIPPEE!

NINE   is a bubble on a stick.

DOKUZ

Dokuz bir çubuk

üstünde baloncuktur.

A BUBBLE! BIR BALONCUK!

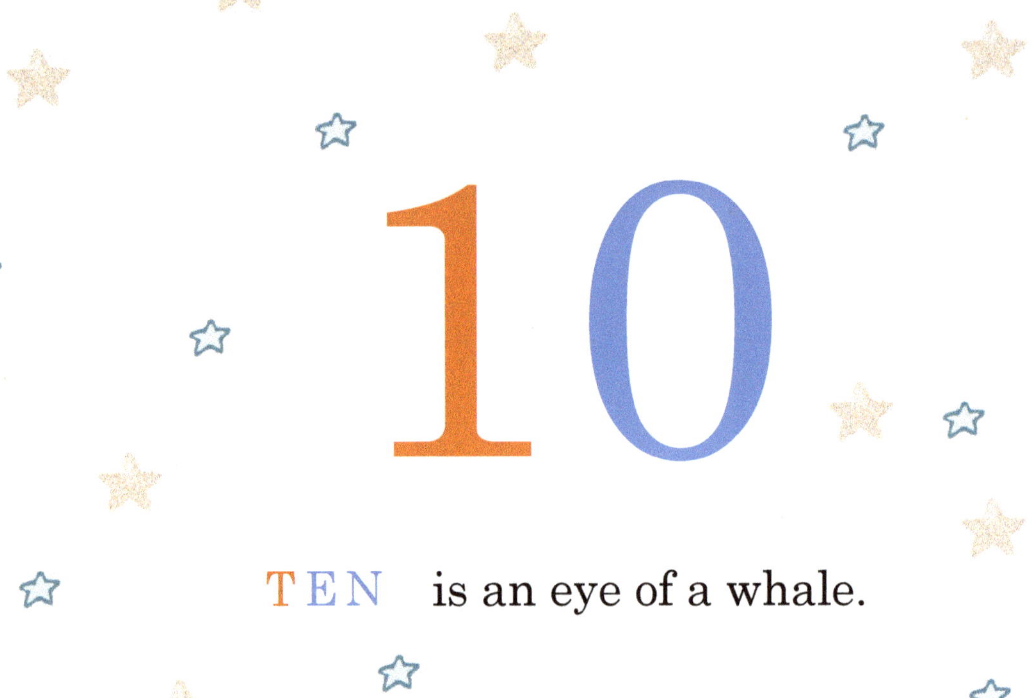

10

TEN   is an eye of a whale.

ON

On balinanın bir gözüdür.

WINK!
Göz kırpıyor!!
HELLO! MERHABA!

And
Ve

0

ZERO   is an empty pail.

SIFIR

Sıfır boş bir kovadır.

IT'S
EMPTY!
BOŞTUR!

Thank you for playing with us today.

We had a lot of fun too!

Bugün bizimle oynadığın için teşekkür ederiz.

Biz de çok eğlendik!

We are your Number friends,
Zero to Ten,
Who will be here for you~
Senin sayı arkadaşlarınız

sıfırdan ona kadar.

Her zaman yanındayız.

Bye-bye now!
See you again soon.

Şimdi güle güle!

Tekrar görüşmek üzere!

The Numbers are *SINGING* too!

To sing-a-long, look for Miss Anna Number Story
at your favorite music store like iTUNES.

MP3

Numbers 0-10
IDENTIFYING
& COUNTING

Numbers 11-20
& Ordinals

first, second, third...

Numbers 0-100
& Place Values

ones, tens, hundreds...

About Clocks
& Telling Time

hours, minutes, seconds

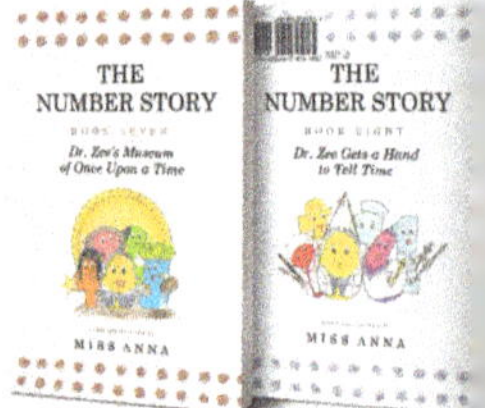

Number Story 1 & 2

isbn: 978-0-996216-48-7

Number Story 3 & 4

isbn: 978-1-945977-01-5

Number Story 5 & 6

isbn: 978-1-945977-06-0

Number Story 7 & 8

isbn: 978-1-949320-40-

For more Miss Anna books to love,
visit us at

www.missannabooks.com

Numbers are working hard all over the world!
Come Travel the World with Us!